New Jersey State Parks

History and Facts

Kevin Woyce

Photographs by the author

Doug Van
Valkenburgh
2011

Kevin Woyce

NEW JERSEY STATE PARKS: HISTORY AND FACTS

ISBN-13: 9780982324028

First Edition: June 2011

For more information, please contact:
Email: kevinwoyce@hotmail.com
Website: kevinwoyce.com

Also available as an e-book.

Front Cover: High Point Monument

Contents

1. Allaire
2. Allamuchy Mountain
3. Barnegat Light
4. Cape May Point
5. Cheesequake
6. Corson's Inlet
7. D&R Canal
8. Double Trouble
9. Farny
10. Fort Mott
11. Hacklebarney
12. High Point
13. Hopatcong
14. Island Beach
15. Kittatinny Valley
16. Liberty
17. Long Pond Ironworks
18. Monmouth Battlefield
19. Parvin
20. Princeton Battlefield
21. Rancocas
22. Ringwood
23. Stephens
24. Swartswood
25. Voorhees
26. Washington Crossing
27. Washington Rock
28. Wawayanda

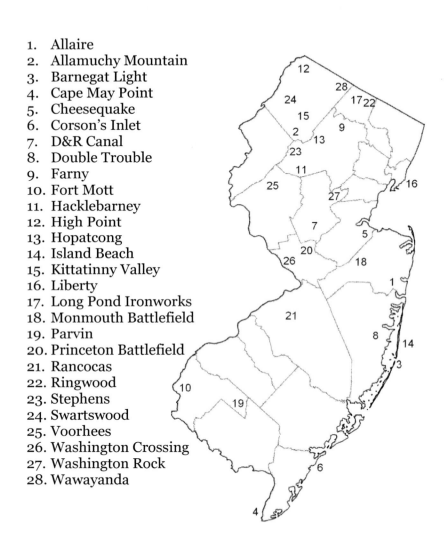

NEW JERSEY STATE PARKS
(Approximate locations)

Introduction

New Jersey is known as the most densely populated state: 8.8 million people in 8721 square miles. It seems everybody has heard about our crowded highways, unsafe cities, and decaying factories.

Like most people who live here, I always knew there was much more to the Garden State. Still, I was surprised to discover that we had 28 state parks, totaling more than 110,000 acres (about 173 square miles). And the diversity! Our state might be small, but the landscapes of our parks range from ocean beaches to mountaintops, wetlands to Pine Barrens.

Until I began researching this book, I assumed that our state parks fell into two categories: obvious historic sites, such as Revolutionary War battlefields; and undeveloped land the State chose to preserve. The truth, of course, is more interesting. Most of our parkland was not bypassed by development. It was mined, quarried, farmed, and stripped of timber. Instead of hiking trails, picnic groves, and swimming lakes, there were iron forges, factory towns, canals, railroads, and private summer resorts.

This is not a guidebook, or a detailed survey of our parks. I have chosen instead to write about history: what occurred on our parklands before they were designated state parks; where some of them got their names; and how some very unlikely places were transformed.

Kevin Woyce

Swartswood State Park: Swan on Swartswood Lake.

Chapter One

State Parks

In the late 1890s, the New Jersey Palisades were being dynamited for stone to build the area's growing cities. One quarry operator near Fort Lee was removing 12,000 tons of rock *every day*.

Elizabeth Vermilye and Cecelia Gaines Holland, members of the Women's Club of Englewood, realized that if the quarrying continued, one of New Jersey's most recognizable landmarks would soon disappear. By 1899, they had created the New Jersey Federation of Women's Clubs, which petitioned Governor Foster Voorhees to stop the blasting.

Voorhees worked with Theodore Roosevelt, then governor of New York, to create the Palisades Interstate Park Commission in 1900. (Voorhees would later donate his 325-acre farm to New Jersey for a state park. Roosevelt became William McKinley's vice president, and was sworn in as president after McKinley's assassination in September 1901. The first conservationist president, Roosevelt quadrupled the size of the nation's forest reserves; used the Antiquities Act of 1906 to establish the first 16 national monuments; and encouraged conservation efforts by the states.)

Kevin Woyce

Palisades Interstate Park: The Lenape Indians called these cliffs *Weehawken*, "rocks that look like trees."

Roosevelt appointed George W. Perkins president of the Commission. His first task, raise enough money—mostly through private donations—to buy the quarries. Perkins, a vice president of the New York Life Insurance Company, appealed to banker J.P. Morgan... and on Christmas Eve, 1900, the Palisades Interstate Park Commission bought out the quarry owners. (Perkins became a partner in Morgan's company in 1905, and helped Roosevelt organize the Progressive Party in 1912.)

The modern park stretches from Fort Lee to Bear Mountain. The first section, from Fort Lee to just north of the New York state line, opened in 1909. By 1919, a million people were visiting every year. In April 1929, the Commission dedicated a stone monument, shaped like a small castle, to the NJ Federation of Women's Clubs.

State-owned parks were a new idea. When the National Conference on State Parks met for the first time, in 1921, only 19 states owned parks. (There are now state parks in all 50 states, for a total of more than 6,000; the oldest is Georgia's Indian Springs State Park, established in 1825.)

The conference was suggested by Stephen Mather, first director of the National Park Service. (We have had National Parks since 1872, when Yellowstone opened, but the National Park Service was not created until 1916.) By the 1920s, every state wanted National Parks for the tourists they attracted. But Mather believed the mission of the NPS was to save places with unique scenery of *national* interest, and to make these places accessible by railroad and highway. Each state, he felt, should then work to preserve sites of more local interest, or to provide recreation areas for its citizens.

Edward Stokes was New Jersey's governor from 1905-1908. He fought to limit the power of railroads and utility companies, worked to improve public education, and recommended that the state begin buying and preserving its dwindling forests. In October 1905, the new Forest Park Reservation Commission made its first purchases, two tracts totaling 970 acres. A 1907 purchase, 5432 acres in Sussex County, became the nucleus of Stokes State Forest.

These woodlands were not "parks" in the modern sense, although visitors were welcome to hike, camp, hunt, or fish. The reservations were expected to pay for themselves, by producing valuable timber year after year. The Commission managed cutting and reforestation efforts, and fought to control—or better still, prevent—the wildfires that consumed thousands of acres annually.

The State began buying parklands in 1914.

Swartswood Lake, in western Sussex County, was named for Anthony Swartwout, who once owned a farm in the area. A captain in the New Jersey Frontier Guard, Swartwout was killed, along with his family, when the French and Indian War spilled into New Jersey from Pennsylvania in 1756.

The hilly land around the lake remained sparsely settled well into the twentieth century. Newton—originally spelled "New Town"—was founded in 1761, and later became a major stop on the Sussex Branch Railroad. The lakeshore town of New Paterson appeared in 1824. By 1852, when the people of New Paterson decided to rename their town after the lake, the lake's name was spelled "Swartswood."

Swartswood became a summer resort in the late 1800s. Entrepreneurs built hotels in the hills around the lake, and their guests launched boats from George Emmons's picnic grove to go fishing.

Newark factory owner Andrew Albright built a lakefront estate in 1888. Ten years later, he began charging fishermen a dollar a day to use the lake. Those who refused to pay, he took to court for trespassing, claiming he owned all the property *underneath* the water. The resort industry began dying in 1900, when Albright successfully defended his property rights in the Court of Errors and Appeals.

In 1906, Governor Stokes recommended that all 108 of New Jersey's freshwater lakes "be set apart as public parks and correctly preserved for the use of the people of the state." To make this possible, a 1907 law authorized the Forest Park Reservation Commission to purchase any land surrounding, or covered by, freshwater lakes or ponds.

Albright died in 1906. His son and daughter sold Swartswood Lake to the state in 1914, the first time the Commission bought land solely for use as a park. Two years later, George Emmons donated 12.5 acres of his old lakefront picnic grove (the foundations of his barn, once used as the park office, are still visible near the parking lot). The park has since grown to 2472 acres, with two lakes for boating and swimming, plus campsites, hiking trails, and picnic tables in the surrounding hills.

The immediate popularity of Swartswood State Park inspired the State to begin buying and developing other parks. Since 1961, many of these efforts have been funded by the New Jersey Green Acres bonds. Originally intended to double the state's publicly-owned open space, Green Acres has so far paid for the purchase, protection, or development of more than 650,000 acres of public land.

Other parks, or sections of parks, have been donated to the state.

An 1870 Delaware River flood washed out the bridge between Port Jervis, New York and Matamoras, Pennsylvania. Two years later, Port Jervis lumber merchant Charles. St. John helped finance the construction of its replacement, a double-spanned suspension bridge designed by John A. Roebling (Roebling also designed the Brooklyn Bridge, which his son William completed in 1883). St. John later served two terms in the United States Congress. In 1888, he built an exclusive lakeside resort atop New Jersey's Kittatinny Mountains. Along with dancing, tennis, and croquet, the resort offered spectacular views of a rocky hilltop, 1803 feet above sea level. Because the State Geological Survey identified this as the highest place in New Jersey, St. John named his resort the High Point Inn.

Charles St. John died in 1891, but the Inn remained open for business until 1908.

Kevin Woyce

High Point State Park: Lake Marcia was named after the fiancée of a state geologist in 1855. In the 1940s, there was a Boy Scout camp on the shore of the lake, near the present bathhouse.

Businessman, philanthropist, and conservationist Anthony Kuser bought the property for a vacation home in 1910. Kuser was president of the South Jersey Gas and Electric Lightning Company, and a director of 50 other companies, including Prudential Life Insurance (founded by his father-in-law, Senator John Fairfield Dryden.) A founding member of the New Jersey Audubon Society, he financed a 1909 expedition to study and catalog the pheasants of the Far East.

Kuser and his wife, Susie, expanded and remodeled the High Point Inn, renaming it Kuser Lodge. In 1923, they donated the Lodge—and 11,000 acres, including High Point itself—to New Jersey for a state park. (The gift had one condition attached: no bird hunting was to be allowed in the park.)

High Point State Park: The Grey Rock Inn, built in 1931 as the park's cafeteria, was designed by Marion Sims Wyeth, architect of the High Point Monument. (Wyeth was best known for building mansions in Palm Beach, Florida, where Anthony Kuser spent his summers after donating High Point.)

Landscaped by the sons of Frederick Law Olmstead, designer of New York's Central Park, High Point State Park quickly became one of New Jersey's most popular destinations. Kuser Lodge was the park office and museum, with eight rooms of exhibits, including collections of New Jersey birds, steamship models, and guns from every American war since the 1700s.

In 1928, Kuser donated half a million dollars for the construction of a monument atop High Point. Modeled after the 1843 Bunker Hill monument, the 220-foot granite tower is dedicated to the "Glory and Honor and Eternal Memory of New Jersey's heroes by Land and Sea and Air in all Wars of our country." Governor Morgan Lewis laid the

Kevin Woyce

cornerstone on June 8, 1828. The monument grew by as much as three feet a day in the summer of 1929, and was completed about a year after Anthony Kuser's death. His son, State Senator John Dryden Kuser, spoke at the dedication ceremony on June 21, 1930.

The four windows at the top of the tower offer some of New Jersey's most impressive views. In the early 1930s, about half of the park's 700,000 annual visitors climbed the 291 spiral stairs for a look (admission cost 25 cents for adults, 10 for children). But the windows also served a practical purpose: at night, when the shaft was illuminated by floodlights, a powerful beacon shone through the windows to guide airplane pilots.

The monument was closed for eight years in the 1990s and early 2000s, after one of its bronze doors was stolen and the stairs were found to be badly corroded by exposure. The damage has been repaired, and the monument is now open most summer weekends.

Kuser Lodge was not so lucky. After decades of neglect, the 37-room mansion was closed to the public in 1977. Restoration plans were scrapped in 1990, due to a lack of funding, and the building was demolished in 1995.

New Jersey's state parks are maintained and operated by the Division of Parks and Forestry, part of the New Jersey Department of Environmental Protection (NJDEP). Several older agencies were combined to form the NJDEP on April 22, 1970—the first "Earth day." In addition to the state parks, the Division of Parks and Forestry also looks after 50 historic sites, 11 state forests, and three recreation areas.

Voorhees State Park: A pair of stone armchairs, facing each other at the top of the Vista Trail.

Franklin D. Roosevelt was elected governor of New York in 1928. In October 1929, the stock market crashed, plunging the nation into the Great Depression. By the start of the 1930s, millions of Americans were unemployed. In 1931, Roosevelt launched an experimental program in New York: he began hiring young, unemployed men to work in the state's forests and parks, fighting fires, planting new trees, and building trails and roads.

Promising Americans a "New Deal," Roosevelt was elected president in 1932. In March 1933, he signed the Emergency Conservation Work Act, creating the Civilian Conservation Corps (CCC). The first CCC camp opened one month later, in Virginia's George Washington National Forest. By July 1933, about 300,000 men were working at 1463 camps. At its height in the mid-1930s, the CCC employed more than half a million men at 2600 camps; 561 of these camps were located in national or state parks.

Most CCC workers were young men, aged 17 to 24. They enrolled for six months, but could remain on the job up to two years. Pay was $30 a month, $25 of which was sent directly to their families. Special companies were formed for veterans, American Indians, and African Americans.

New Jersey had 22 camps. Five were in state forests, two in state parks.

Camp #20 opened at Voorhees State Park in October 1933, and remained in operation until June 1941. The park is named after Foster Voorhees, who served in the New Jersey House of Representatives and the State Senate before being elected governor in 1899. When he died in 1927, Voorhees left his Hill Acres farm to the state.

The CCC demolished the old farm buildings, planted evergreens on the cleared fields, and built trails, fireplaces, and shelters that are still in use. Workers from "Camp Voorhees" also helped to develop nearby Hacklebarney State Park, building parking lots, drinking fountains, bridges, and stairs.

Before building High Point's campsites, Corps workers had to transform a cedar swamp into Sawmill Lake. They also built the popular Monument Trail.

Stephens State Park: Donated to New Jersey in 1937, the park stretches for a mile along the Musconetcong River. Workers from a CCC camp in Hackettstown planted trees, bridged the river, and built picnic tables and benches.

Parvin State Park, in southwestern New Jersey, is named for Elemuel Parvin, who bought the property in 1793. Today's Parvin Lake had been created just 10 years earlier, when a previous owner dammed the steam known as Muddy Run to power his sawmill. Parvin and his descendants ran the mill until the late 1800s, when they sold the land to a resort operator. (The Parvin house still stands, but is closed to visitors. The mill, long known as the Coombs Ackley Mill—Ackley married Parvin's great-granddaughter Jane in 1849—was demolished in the 1930s.)

Kevin Woyce

Parvin State Park: CCC workers built the bathhouse complex in 1939, reusing bricks from demolished Philadelphia buildings.

The property's new owner renamed it Union Grove, built a sand beach and a concession stand, and rented boats to visitors. His son lost a fortune when the stock market crashed in '29, and sold the park to the state to pay off his debt.

Parvin State Park opened on September 12, 1931. Two years later, CCC Company 1225 moved into camp "SP-4." They built campsites, trails, and pavilions, many of which are still in use, and began transforming a swamp into "Thundergust Lake." In 1937, Company 1225 moved to Nevada, and a company of WWI veterans took their place at Parvin. Company 2227V finished digging the new lake and built rental cabins and bridges. When a September flood destroyed the old dam in 1940, they built a concrete replacement.

Parvin State Park: Parvin Lake Dam.

The camp closed in May 1942.The buildings were briefly used to house wartime workers, and then German prisoners of war. In the early 1950s, Kalmyk refugees from the Soviet Union lived here until they found permanent homes in New Jersey and Pennsylvania. (The Kalmyk, descended from Mongolian nomads, were unable to return to their homeland because Stalin falsely accused them of collaborating with the Germans during WWII.) Today, all that remains of the camp is a stone chimney in the woods.

The Civilian Conservation Corps was disbanded in 1942, when the United States began mobilizing for the Second World War. During its brief life, the Corps provided temporary jobs for 2.5 million men; it has since inspired the Job Corps Civilian Conservation Centers of the 1960s, the Youth Conservation Corps of the 1970s, and many regional conservation efforts.

Kevin Woyce

Parvin State Park: The 1937 "White Bridge" is one of several wooden bridges CCC workers built over the park's waterways.

The Works Progress Administration (later renamed the Works Projects Administration) provided eight million jobs between 1935 and 1943. Another of Roosevelt's New Deal agencies, the WPA is mostly remembered for building roads and public buildings, such as libraries and firehouses. But WPA workers also dug three lakes at Cheesequake State Park, and built trails at Washington Crossing.

Voorhees State Park: The Paul H. Robinson Observatory, attached to the Edwin Aldrin Astronomical Center (Robinson is one of the seven founders of the New Jersey Astronomical Association (NJAA); NJ native "Buzz" Aldrin landed on the moon in 1969).

The dome houses a 26-inch telescope, built for Indiana University in the 1930s and moved to New Jersey in 1965.

The 3M Corporation sponsored the installation of a "Solar System Trail" near the observatory in 2002. The trail is a scale model of our solar system, beginning at a sign representing the sun and marked with signs describing each planet. Students from the Voorhees High School Astronomy Club, which helped design the signs, measured the relative distances between the sun and its planets.

For observatory hours, visit njaa.org.

Hopatcong State Park: Lake Hopatcong.

Chapter Two

Lenape

According to the 1905 tourist guide *Lake Hopatcong Illustrated*, "the name Hopatcong is an Indian word meaning honey water of many coves."

This is partly true. Hopatcong is, in fact, derived from "an Indian word," *hapakonoesson*. But the "many coves" translation was invented by real estate promoters, eager to sell building lots on the lake's 45 miles of shoreline. Historians believe the real meaning is "pipestone," and refers to nearby deposits of the soft steatite, or "soapstone," that Native Americans carved pipes from.

In the 1500s, all of New Jersey, plus parts of eastern Pennsylvania, southeastern New York, and northern Delaware, was *Lenapehoking*, "Land of the Lenape." The Lenni-Lenape, or "Original People," were New Jersey's earliest settlers. Because they arrived about 10,000 years ago, after a slow migration from the cold northwest, neighboring tribes called them "grandfathers" or "the ancient ones."

They lived in the woods, usually in groups of 25 or 30; only the largest towns had populations of more than 200. They hunted, fished, and raised corn, beans and squash. Some groups spent their summers along the shore, gathering shellfish from the ocean beaches. Among Native Americans, they were known as expert traders and peacemakers.

Contact with white traders and settlers proved disastrous. European diseases destroyed whole villages. Misunderstandings with the Dutch lead to wars in the 1640s. When the land-hungry British conquered New Netherland in 1664, Lenape bands began moving north and west out of New Jersey. Their descendants settled as far away as Oklahoma and Canada.

In 1758, the Lenape signed away their rights to New Jersey. Most had already left the colony. Christian missionaries settled 100 families on the Brotherton Reservation, deep in the Pine Barrens. They did not remain long. In 1802, the "Brotherton Indians" sold their reservation to cover the cost of moving to a Mohican settlement in New Stockbridge, New York.

Other Lenape families remained in New Jersey, living quietly in isolated communities, secretly keeping their traditions alive while hiding their identity from outsiders. Joining them were the Nanticoke, who began migrating into New Jersey from southern Delaware in the 1600s.

(Although both Lenape and Nanticoke are sometimes called "Delaware Indians," *Delaware* is not a native word. The river was named after Lord De La Warre, governor of Jamestown Colony in 1610-11.)

The Nanticoke Lenni-Lenape Tribe incorporated in 1978, following the passage of the American Indian Religious Freedom Act. Recognized by the State of New Jersey, they operate a museum and a trading post at their headquarters in Bridgeton, and hold a weekend-long powwow every June.

Like many of New Jersey's rivers, towns, and mountains, several state parks have Lenape names.

Kittatinny Valley State Park: The Visitor's Center is an 1825 farmhouse, enlarged by Aeroflex founder Fred Hussey. Park volunteers maintain a butterfly and hummingbird garden behind the house.

Kittatinny Valley State Park is named for the Kittatinny Mountains. Part of the 2,000 mile Appalachian chain, their name means "endless mountain."

New Jersey acquired the park in 1994, with Green Acres money. Fifty years earlier, Fred Hussey bought most of the property from the YMCA, which had been using it for a boys' camp since 1919. Hussey was founder and president of the Aeroflex Corporation, which made gyroscopic cameras for warplanes during WWII, and now specializes in microelectronics and high-tech testing equipment.

Hacklebarney State Park: Black River waterfall.

Hussey moved the Aeroflex headquarters to his mountain estate and built a private airport, with a 2,000 foot runway, alongside New Jersey's deepest glacial lake (110 feet). The lake is now called Lake Aeroflex, and the New Jersey Forest Fire Service maintains Aeroflex-Andover Airport.

Hacklebarney State Park may owe its name to a Lenape word for "bonfire."

Adolphe Edward Borie, president of the Savage Arms Company and a vice president of Bethlehem Steel, donated the first 35 acres in 1924, another 90 in 1929. He dedicated the park to "two women of rare vision, character, and courage:" his mother, Susan Parke Borie; and his niece, Susan Ryerson Patterson.

Susan Patterson survived the *Titanic* disaster in 1912, and then spent the First World War in France, earning the French *Croix De Guerre* (Cross of War) and *Medaille de la Reconnaissance* (Medal of Recognition) for her work on the front as a nurse. She was just 30 years old when she died in 1921, struck down by heart failure after an appendectomy.

There is a Wawayanda Lake and a Wawayanda Mountain, but the Lenape first gave this musical name (pronounced "way-way-yonda") to the creek that feeds the lake. It is usually translated as "Winding Water" or "Wandering River."

Sumner Dudley, "the fathering of YMCA camping," started the nation's first summer camp on Wawayanda's Twin Islands in 1886. The camp soon outgrew the islands, and was moved to Andover, and then to Lake Champlain, where it still operates as Camp Dudley.

Kevin Woyce

Wawayanda State Park: View from the Lake Wawayanda beach.

YMCA camping returned to Wawayanda in 1901, when a cable-drawn ferry was built to First Island. After 1919, Camp Wawayanda moved several times before finding a permanent home at Frost Valley, in the Catskill Mountains.

New Jersey bought the lake and 440 acres in 1960, adding another 10,000 acres with Green Acres funding in 1963. Wawayanda is now our largest state park, covering more than 34,000 acres (the next largest, High Point, is less than half this size: 15,827 acres). Crossing Wawayanda on the Appalachian Trail is a 20 mile hike.

Allamuchy Mountain State Park: Jefferson Lake, photographed from the Sussex Branch Trail.

According to George Wyckoff Cummins's 1911 *History of Allamuchy, NJ*, the name *Allamuchy* has been in use since 1715, when deputy surveyor John Reading explored the banks of the Pequest River for William Penn. (Penn was the Quaker founder of Pennsylvania, and one of the few early settlers to deal fairly with the Lenape. The Pequest is a 25-mile tributary of the Delaware.) In one of his letters to Penn, Reading mentioned a Lenape village he called *Allamucha*. Shortened from the name of the local chief, *Allamuchahokkingen*, the name means "place within the hills."

In Allamuchy Mountain State Park, there is a reproduction of a Lenape settlement called *Wikakung* ("Place of Sassafras"), with wood and bark wigwams and longhouses. For many years, it was open to the public as part of Waterloo Village. Visiting in the 1990s, I saw a demonstration of how the Lenape carved dugout canoes. Unfortunately, Waterloo has been closed for several years, following a failed attempt at privatization. As of 2010, the Lenape village was only open for school tours.

Cheesequake State Park: Hooks Creek Lake is the largest of the park's three lakes, all of which were dug by WPA workers in 1941.

Lenape settlements in the hills above a creek flowing into Raritan Bay were called *Cheseh-oh-ke*, meaning "upland village" or "upland people." Later settlers, who planted farms and built pottery factories in the hills, mistook the Lenape word for the name of the creek. They also misspelled it "Cheesequake," much to the amusement of generations of Parkway drivers (the Garden State Parkway crosses the park).

New Jersey bought 735 acres in 1938. Cheesequake State Park opened two years later, after the WPA cleared away the farm buildings and built roads, trails, and parking lots. The Parkway cut through in 1955.

Rancocas State Park: World Championship Hoop Dancer Daniel Tramper, performing at the May 2010 American Indian Arts Festival.

Settlers named Rancocas Creek, a 30-mile tributary of the Delaware, after the Ankokus, a sub tribe of the Lenape who lived along its banks. The modern spelling may be a result of the old mapmakers' habit of placing an "R." before the names of rivers.

The Creek flows through Rancocas State Park, which the state purchased in 1965. In 1982, The Powhatan Renape Nation began leasing the 280-acre Rankokus Indian Reservation. For the next 28 years, they ran a museum and hosted Juried American Indian Arts Festivals

31

every May and October. The May, 2010 event featured music, food, dancing, storytelling, and art from all parts of the Americas; a Mexican troupe presented traditional Aztec dances.

In September 2010, the NJDEP reclaimed all but five acres.

Renape is an Algonquian word meaning "human beings." *Powhatan* was the name of a group of 30 tribes united under a single chief in the late 1500s. They met the British at Jamestown, and by 1644, their power was shattered, their numbers cut down by wars and disease. Virginia now recognizes seven nations made up of their descendants.

Other Powhatan began settling in southwestern New Jersey in the late 1800s. Like the Nanticoke and Lenape, they kept their heritage a secret until the 1970s. New Jersey officially recognized them as the Powhatan Renape Nation in 1980.

The museum will remain open, and the Powhatan will continue to perform religious ceremonies on their sacred mound. But their buffalo has been moved to Great Adventure, and they will have to apply for permits to hold future Festivals within the park.

Cooper's Gristmill: Nathan Cooper built this mill in 1826, on the site a 1760s flour mill. Located on the Black River near Hacklebarney State Park, it is now a museum operated by the Morris County Park Commission.

33

Trenton Battle Monument

Chapter Three

Revolution

The British captured New York in the fall of 1776, and held the city until 1783. The American colonists made Philadelphia their wartime capital. Trapped between these two strongholds, New Jersey became known as the "Crossroads of the American Revolution." More battles and skirmishes were fought here than in any other state. Four state parks, a National Historical Park, and dozens of monuments and markers celebrate these difficult years.

George Washington ferried the last remnants of his army across the Delaware River to Pennsylvania on December 8, 1776. Costly defeats on Long Island and Manhattan had left him just 3,000 dispirited volunteers, many of whom planned to quit when their enlistments expired on New Year's Eve.

Only two things saved them from a British attack. First, Washington had his men hide or destroy every boat on the New Jersey side of the Delaware. Second, the British Commander-in-Chief, Sir William Howe, ordered his men off the pursuit and into winter quarters. The redcoats did not fight in winter, and Howe believed that the harsh weather alone would destroy the ragged Continental Army.

But as the British settled down for the winter, Washington made plans to "clip their wings." The addition of fresh Pennsylvania troops, Philadelphia militia, and New England veterans commanded by Benedict Arnold swelled his army to 6,000 men.

Kevin Woyce

Washington Crossing State Park: Modern reproduction of one of the wooden boats Washington used to cross the Delaware in 1776. The 1904 Washington Crossing Bridge is visible in the background.

On Christmas night, Washington divided his troops into three columns. Each would attempt to cross the icy Delaware aboard wooden ferries and flat-bottomed cargo boats. An hour before dawn, all three columns were to attack Trenton, which Howe had entrusted to a small force of German mercenaries.

Only one column, the 2500 men commanded by Washington himself, actually landed in New Jersey. Hauling 18 artillery pieces nine miles through a snowstorm took longer than planned, so they did not arrive in Trenton until after daylight.

Still, their arrival was unexpected, and the Germans had neglected to fortify a strategic hill. Washington placed his guns there instead, and ordered a young Alexander Hamilton to fire down into the city. In less than an hour, the fighting was over. Washington quickly marched his troops back to McConkey's ferry, along with 900 prisoners and a valuable collection of guns, horses, and wagons. By the time they returned to their camps in Pennsylvania, some of his men had been awake for 50 hours and marched 40 miles.

At the start of January, they were back in Trenton. Washington had offered his troops $10 apiece to fight another six weeks, and most had accepted. When Sir William Howe sent Lord Cornwallis with 6,000 men to recapture Trenton, the Continental Army met them at Assunpink Creek. Delayed by American riflemen in the woods, the redcoats arrived late in the afternoon. Three times they attacked the American lines; three times they were driven back. Cornwallis decided to rest his men overnight and attack the Americans in the morning.

Washington took the opportunity to launch another surprise attack. Leaving their tents in place and their campfires burning, the Continental Army marched overnight to attack the British garrison at Princeton. The weather slowed them, as it had Christmas night. Once again, they arrived later than Washington had planned. But the British at Princeton were just as surprised as the Germans had been at Trenton. Within 15 minutes, the redcoats were on the run.

Instead of trying his luck by attacking the British stores and gold at New Brunswick—his original objective this morning—Washington marched his battered army to Morristown, where they dug in for the winter. Surprised by Washington's cunning, and wary of ambushes in the New Jersey woods, Cornwallis let them escape. Like Howe, he expected the winter to finish them off.

Kevin Woyce

Washington Crossing Historic Park (Pennsylvania): Before crossing the Delaware on Christmas night, George Washington dined with his officers at McConkey's Ferry Inn.

Historians refer to this brief period of Washington's career as the "Ten Crucial Days," when a single misstep could have destroyed his Army and lost the war.

Washington's Crossing National Historic Landmark, established in 1961, includes parks on both sides of the Delaware. When New Jersey's Washington Crossing State Park opened in 1912, it was just 100 acres overlooking McConkey's ferry crossing. Greatly expanded and developed by the WPA in the 1930s, the park now includes several historic buildings, walking trails, and a museum housing more than 600 Revolutionary War artifacts.

Pennsylvania's Washington Crossing Historic Park includes the riverfront McConkey's Ferry Inn, which Washington used as a watch post, and where he dined before the Christmas night crossing. When he reached New

Jersey, he coordinated the landings and the march to Trenton from the Johnson Ferry House, the oldest building in Washington Crossing State Park.

A reproduction of one of the flat-bottomed wooden boats Washington used for the crossings rests outside another ferryman's cottage, nearer the river. Called "Durham boats," they were built to ferry coal and iron ore between colonial mines and forges. Additional reproductions are stored on the Pennsylvania side, for the annual Christmas day reenactment.

The Delaware is about 800 feet wide here, and was first bridged in 1832. The present steel-frame Washington Crossing Bridge was built in 1904, after a flood carried away the old wooden span. Park visitors can cross on the wooden sidewalk alongside the narrow roadway.

The cornerstone of the Trenton Battle Monument was set on December 26, 1891—115 years after the battle. Two years later, the monument was finished: a 148-foot granite column, topped by a 13-foot bronze statue of George Washington. Bronze relief panels on the base show "The Continental Army Crossing the Delaware River," "Opening of the Battle," and "Surrender of the Hessians." A smaller plaque immortalizes the bitter words of Britain's Colonial Secretary of State, Lord Germain: "All our hopes were blasted by that unhappy affair at Trenton."

Twenty thousand people, including the governors of eight of the first 13 states, attended the monument's dedication on October 19, 1893—the 112th anniversary of Washington's victory at Yorktown.

The monument is considered part of Washington Crossing State Park, though it stands nine miles south of the park at the top of North Warren and North Broad Streets in Trenton. (Before Washington placed the

American artillery there, the streets were named King and Queen.)

Some of the fiercest fighting at Princeton occurred on Thomas Clarke's 200 acre farm. Although the property was divided and sold several times before the state purchased it in 1946, the 85-acre Princeton Battlefield State Park once included two important reminders of the battle.

The first is Thomas Clarke's 1772 house, where wounded soldiers from both armies were treated after the battle. The second was a large oak tree in the middle of the battlefield. According to legend, American general Hugh Mercer rested against the tree after being bayoneted by British soldiers. Only when the fighting was finished would he allow himself to be carried to the farmhouse, where he died nine days later.

The Clarke House is now a Revolutionary War museum, but the famed Mercer Oak is no more. A windstorm ripped the last branches from the 300-year-old tree in March 2000. After the ruined trunk was cut down, a sapling grown from one of the oak's acorns was planted inside the stump.

The park's most unusual landmark is a stone colonnade, facing the Clarke House from a hilltop on the opposite side of Mercer Road. Designed by Thomas U. Walter, architect of the Senate and House wings of the U.S. Capitol building, it was originally the entrance to a private home in Philadelphia. The colonnade was moved to Princeton in 1900, as the front porch of a mansion called Mercer Manor. After the Manor burned in the 1950s, the building's owner donated the columns to the State of New Jersey. They were declared a National Historic Landmark in 1962.

Princeton Battlefield State Park:
Top: Thomas Clarke House. *Bottom:* Ionic Colonnade.

41

Kevin Woyce

Part of the encampment where Washington's army spent the frigid winter of 1777 has been preserved as the Morristown National Historic Park.

In the spring of 1777, Washington stretched his army along the top of the Watchung Mountains, blocking the land routes between New York and Philadelphia. Militia guarded the passes at Middlebrook, Stoney Brook, and Scotch Plains. Howe dared not attack the mountains, and Washington refused to be drawn down into battle. In July, Washington watched from the mountains as the British Army abandoned New Jersey aboard 270 warships.

Washington kept his army in the mountains until mid-August, when he heard that the warships were approaching Philadelphia. He then pulled together 11,000 troops, and attempted to block the much larger British force at Brandywine Creek. On September 11, he was forced to retreat. The British occupied Philadelphia on September 23, and held the American capital until June 1778.

For several decades in the late 1800s, a rocky outcrop atop the Watching Mountains was whitewashed every year, so it would be visible for miles around. A plaque at the base of the flagpole monument in Washington Rock State Park explains why:

"From this Rock General George Washington watched the movements of the British Forces during the anxious months of May and June 1777."

Chances are, this was not Washington's only lookout during those months. The earliest drawing of "Washington Rock," from Benson J. Lossing's 1851 *Field Book of the Revolution*, shows a different rock entirely.

Washington Rock State Park: Scenic overlook created by the Daughters of the American Revolution in 1912.

Still, Green Brook families have passed down the story that Washington was lead here by a local farmer since the 1700s. The area around the rock has been a popular picnic grove since the 1840s. On July 4, 1851, more than 2,000 people gathered to celebrate our nation's 75th birthday. A three story hotel, the Washington Rock House, opened the following year, and stagecoach service began in the 1870s. On July 4, 1867, the Washington Monument and Historical State Association laid the cornerstone for a 100-foot observation tower.

The tower was never completed. Developers built hotels and summer cottages in the surrounding hills, but the Rock itself almost vanished. In 1909, the McCutcheon family of North Plainfield bought the lookout to save it from a quarrying company. Four years later, they sold the Rock and 27 acres of woodland to New Jersey for $1.

Washington Rock State Park opened in 1913, featuring two impressive monuments built by the Continental Chapter of the Daughters of the American Revolution. One is a tall flagpole, whose stone base rests on the foundation of the never-built observation tower. The other is an 80-foot long stone wall connecting the park's two outcrops, Washington Rock and its smaller neighbor, Lafayette Rock. The State added a caretaker's cottage in 1914.

The British evacuated Philadelphia on June 18, 1778. Heavy guns and loyalist refugees left by ship. Fifteen thousand troops began marching northeast across New Jersey, toward the fleet gathering at Sandy Hook. Howe's successor as Commander-in-Chief, Henry Clinton, planned to win the war by defending New York and invading the southern colonies.

Nine days into the march, a reinvigorated Continental Army caught up with the British at Monmouth Courthouse. Washington sent his second-in-command, General Charles Lee, to attack them on the morning of June 28. Lee, doubting the wisdom of the attack, ordered a retreat when the British fought back. Luckily, Washington was following with a larger force, and was able to turn his fleeing soldiers around for a second attempt.

Monmouth Battlefield State Park:
Above: Fences marking the location of British artillery during the battle.
Page 44: Statue of Baron Von Steuben.

This was a new Continental Army. Starting in 1777, new recruits were signed up for "three years or until the end of the war." Baron Von Steuben, a Prussian volunteer, spent the long winter training and drilling them at Valley Forge, Pennsylvania.

The armies faced each other across farmers' fields and orchards, trading artillery volleys in hundred-degree heat. When one of the American gunners was wounded, his wife, Mary Hays, took his place on the gun crew (in the 1700s, soldiers' wives often accompanied their men, helping with the cooking and laundry). History has nicknamed her "Molly Pitcher" because she spent most of the afternoon carrying water from a spring to her husband's artillery regiment. In the heat of the battle, soldiers shouted, "Molly, Pitcher!"

Kevin Woyce

Late in the afternoon, General Nathaniel Green, one of Washington's most trusted advisors, moved four guns to a hilltop overlooking the battlefield. When his fire scattered the British artillery, the newly trained Continental infantry drove the redcoats from the field. This time, it was the British who marched away after dark; in the morning, they sailed out of New Jersey.

Monmouth Battlefield was named a National Historic Landmark in 1961. The 3,000 acre Monmouth Battlefield State Park opened in 1978, the 200th anniversary of the battle. There is a statue of Von Steuben outside the Visitor's Center, on the hilltop where Greene placed the American guns. and sSeveral springs in the park have been named after "Molly Pitcher." Since 1990, the nonprofit Friends of Monmouth Battlefield have helped to restore, maintain, and interpret the park. Each June, they host a weekend-long reenactment of the battle, which many historians consider the "turning point" of the Revolution.

The British captured both New York and Philadelphia by sailing large fleets of warships into poorly defended harbors. To prevent this from happening in future wars, the United States Army built a long chain of masonry forts along the eastern seaboard and around the entrances to major rivers.

In 1886, a committee chaired by William Endicott, Grover Cleveland's Secretary of War, declared most of these forts inadequate defense against modern naval guns. To fully protect our shores, the "Endicott Board" recommended building new forts at 29 locations.

One of these was Finn's Point, on the New Jersey side of Delaware Bay. The Army had bought land for a battery in the 1830s, but did not begin building until 1872. Already obsolete, the fort was left unfinished.

46

Fort Mott State Park: Only the iron watch towers rise above the fort's earthworks and concealed batteries.

An "Endicott Period" fort was begun in 1896, in anticipation of the Spanish-American War. It was named the following year, after Major General Gershom Mott, a New Jersey veteran of both the Mexican-American and the Civil War. After retiring from the Army, Mott served as New Jersey's State Treasurer, and as Commander of the New Jersey National Guard.

Unlike earlier forts, Endicott defenses were meant to be invisible from the water. Concrete batteries were hidden behind high mounds of earth, designed to absorb naval shells that would have shattered masonry walls. The biggest guns, able to lob thousand pound projectiles eight miles across the water, were raised and lowered by steam engines, so they were only exposed when firing. A moat protected the batteries from attack by land.

Kevin Woyce

Fort Mott State Park: The ferry dock, photographed from the top of Fort Mott. Fort Delaware is in the background.

Fort Mott was manned from 1897 until 1922, but its guns were never fired except for testing and practice. All the artillery was removed by 1943, when the fort was declared "surplus property." New Jersey bought it in 1947, and opened Fort Mott State Park in June, 1951. The concrete batteries are open for walking tours year round. Summer visitors can also ride ferries to Fort Delaware, an 1859 fortress and Civil War prison on Pea Patch Island, near the mouth of the Delaware River. (The island is believed to be haunted, by the ghosts of Confederate soldiers who died there during the war.)

Allaire State Park: The Howell Iron Works' Company Store was once New Jersey's largest retail building. Now called the General Store, it is part of the Historic Village at Allaire.

Double Trouble State Park: Cedar Creek. The rivers and swamps of the Pine Barrens, located in central and southern New Jersey, were rich sources of bog iron.

Chapter Four

Iron

There is so much iron dissolved in the rivers and streams of central New Jersey, that along with decaying leaves, it colors their water reddish brown. In the swamps and bogs of the Pine Barrens, bacteria converts the dissolved iron to thin layers of rust, which then combine with sand and clay to form lumps of ore. Although this "bog iron" is a low grade ore—only about 30% iron—it is relatively easy to find, and can be gathered by hand. Better still, nature is always creating more; the same bogs can be mined every 25 to 30 years.

Early settlers made their tools, pots, and railings from bog iron. During the Revolution, it was used for cannonballs. In the 1830s, James Peter Allaire turned it into one of New Jersey's biggest industries.

Allaire began working in a New York brass foundry in 1802, when he was just 17. Four years later, he opened his own foundry. One of his first customers was Robert Fulton, who hired him to make parts for the steamboat *Clermont*.

Fulton soon had a small fleet of steamboats carrying passengers and cargo up and down the Hudson River. A few months before his death in 1815, Fulton hired Allaire to build the engine for his largest steamboat, the *Chancellor Livingston*. The engine took a year to build, but it made the *Chancellor* the fastest boat on the river.

Kevin Woyce

Allaire State Park: Howell Iron Works blast furnace.

Allaire State Park: A row of ironworkers' houses has been converted to park offices and a museum.

To build the engine, Allaire opened New York's first marine engine factory, the Allaire Iron Works. As the business grew, he knew his continued success would depend on finding a reliable source of inexpensive iron.

His friend Benjamin Howell found the answer in 1821: a 30-year-old Pine Barrens blast furnace. Allaire bought the furnace, and 5,000 acres of woods and wetlands, the following year, for $19,000. He renamed the property Howell Iron Works in 1823, and soon bought another 3,000 acres. The swamps provided ore; wood from the forests could be burned for charcoal to fuel the furnace.

Gathering and refining the low grade ore also required a large workforce, up to 600 men in the 1830s. Many of them lived on Company property, in the brick row houses Allaire began building in 1829. By 1836, Howell Iron

Works was a self-sufficient village of more than 60 buildings, with its own church, school, Post Office, and currency.

Allaire left little to chance. He owned the stagecoaches that hauled iron bars ("pig iron") to Eatontown and Red Bank, and the small fleet of steamships that delivered them to his Manhattan factory. But the economy crashed in 1837, plunging the nation into a five year depression, complete with bank failures and widespread unemployment. Before the nation recovered in the 1840s, high grade ore was discovered in Pennsylvania. Unable to compete, Allaire closed the Howell blast furnace in 1846, and retired in 1850.

He had moved his wife and children to the property's 1790 farmhouse in 1832, after a cholera epidemic struck New York. When he died in 1858, Allaire left the house and property to his second wife, Calicia, and their only child, Hal. Hal lived at the ironworks the rest of his life, alone after Calicia died in 1876.

Newspaper columnist Arthur Brisbane bought the crumbling "Deserted Village" in 1907.

Brisbane was the most popular columnist of his day, syndicated in 1200 newspapers and read by 30 million people every week. He built Manhattan's Ritz Tower and Ziegfeld Theatre, and leased the old Howell Iron Works to the Monmouth County Boy Scouts, who restored some of the abandoned buildings. In 1941, Brisbane's widow donated the land to New Jersey.

The nonprofit "Historic Village at Allaire" has maintained the park's buildings, including Allaire's farmhouse and chapel, since 1957. The last surviving row of workers' houses has been transformed into park offices and a museum, and visitors can still shop at the old Howell Company Store (now renamed the General Store). There is also a blacksmith's shop, and a bakery. The Village hosts dozens of events throughout the year, including concerts, plays, craft fairs, and historical reenactments.

Most of New Jersey's iron is found in the northern part of the state, in narrow bands stretched along the mountain ranges. To find it, dozens of companies dug hundreds of exploratory shafts in the 18th and 19th centuries. Wherever the ore was concentrated, these shafts were expanded into working mines, some of them more than a mile deep. In the richest mines, the ore contained more than 60% iron, twice as much as bog ore.

By the 1870s, mining companies were removing more than half a million tons of ore every year. In their busiest year ever, 1882, they dug out more than 930,000 tons.

The iron had to be melted from the ore in stone blast furnaces. Charcoal fueled the fires until the 1830s, when canals and railroads began delivering anthracite coal from Pennsylvania. To make charcoal, iron companies cut and burned almost every tree in Sussex County between the late 1700s and early 1800s. (Remains of New Jersey's last charcoal furnace, built in 1862 and used for only a few years, are visible near Farny State Park, below Split Rock Reservoir.)

In the 1880s, there were more than 350 iron mines in New Jersey. Though many were inactive, some had been producing ore since before the American Revolution. One of the oldest was Andover Mine, located on property William Penn purchased in 1714. (It was while surveying this tract, in 1715, that John Reading coined the name *Allamuchy*.)

Kevin Woyce

Stephens State Park: Lime Kiln, used to extract quicklime from mountain limestone. Quicklime was mixed with iron ore in blast furnaces. Heated to around 2000 degrees Fahrenheit, the quicklime drew impurities from the ore, creating "slag," which floated on top of the heavier molten iron. The slag was skimmed from the top twice a day, and the iron was molded into rough bars called "pigs."

William Allen and Joseph Turner built Andover Forge in 1763 (the name probably refers to Joseph Turner's English birthplace). When the American Revolution began in 1775, both men remained loyal to England. Three years later, the Continental Congress ordered New Jersey to confiscate the forge. For the rest of the war, Andover made gun barrels and cannons for Washington's army.

The government abandoned Andover in 1783. The mine's postwar owners quickly declared bankruptcy, because they could not afford to ship their iron to Philadelphia's factories. Before railroads and canals, iron had to be hauled overland in horse-drawn wagons to the Delaware, and then loaded onto flat-bottomed "Durham

56

boats" for the trip across. By the 1840s, Andover's mines and forges were nearly forgotten.

Peter Cooper built *Tom Thumb*, America's first steam locomotive, in 1830, to convince the owners of the new Baltimore and Ohio Railroad to use steam power instead of horses. Over the next decade, Cooper made his fortune selling the B&O iron rails.

Cooper never tired of innovation. His forges were the first to burn anthracite coal instead of charcoal. He brought Sir Henry Bessemer's method of purifying steel to America in 1856, just a year after Bessemer introduced it in England. In 1858, he was president of the New York, Newfoundland, and London Telegraph Company, supervising the laying of the first transatlantic telegraph cable.

Cooper was also a social reformer and philanthropist, campaigning against slavery before the Civil War and defending the rights of Native Americans in the 1870s. A lifelong supporter of public education, he opened Cooper Union, a free, coeducational New York college of science, technology, and art, in 1859.

In the early 1840s, Cooper hired Abram Hewitt, a recent Columbia graduate, to tutor his son Edward. The two young men became lifelong friends and business partners, founding the Trenton Iron Company in 1845. Later in life, both were elected mayor of New York: Edward Cooper in 1879; Hewitt in 1886. Hewitt also served four terms in the US Congress.

Like Peter Cooper's first iron mills, the Trenton Iron Company specialized in making railroad rails. Needing a steady supply of high grade ore, Cooper and Hewitt bought the Andover Mine in 1848, for just $2500. By the 1850s, they were removing 3,000 tons every month and shipping it on the newly enlarged Morris Canal. They operated the mine until the ore ran out in 1863, and then sold it a few years later.

Cornelius Board started the Ringwood Iron Works in 1742, and sold the business two years later. The property was then bought and sold several times before Robert Erskine arrived in 1871. During the Revolution, Erskine manufactured guns for the Continental Army and forged an enormous chain to block the Hudson River. He also drew maps for George Washington, who visited the ironworks during the war and attended Erskine's funeral in 1880. (Robert Erskine is buried in his family's cemetery, near Ringwood Manor.)

Martin Ryerson bought the property in 1807, manufactured artillery for the War of 1812, and built himself a 10-room mansion. After he died in 1832, his sons fell into debt. Peter Cooper and Abram Hewitt bought the 22,000 acre ironworks at auction in 1853, for $100,000. They worked the biggest mine until 1879, when extensive ore deposits were discovered around the Great Lakes. The last Ringwood mines were closed in the 1950s.

Abram Hewitt married Sarah Amelia Cooper, Peter's only daughter, in 1855. Sarah fell in love with Ryerson's Manor, and she and her husband spent the rest of their lives remodeling and enlarging it for their growing family (they eventually had six children). By 1936, when the Hewitt family donated the Manor to New Jersey, it had 51 rooms, 24 fireplaces, and more than 250 windows. Ringwood State Park visitors can see some of the forge's products, including links from the Hudson River chain, in front of the house.

Ringwood State Park: Ringwood Manor.

Much of the iron dug from Ringwood was processed at the nearby Long Pond Ironworks, which Peter Hasenclever started in 1766 (Long Pond is the Colonial name for Greenwood Lake). Sent from London by the new American Iron Company, which bought Ringwood in 1764, Hasenclever opened 53 mines and built a small city of furnaces, mills, shops, and barracks. To finish all this in less than two years, he imported more than 500 German workers and their families.

Concerned by his spending, the American Iron Company appointed a replacement and recalled Hasenclever to London, where he declared bankruptcy a few years later. In 1773, he published an account of his works, and of the legal and financial difficulties that followed:

The remarkable case of Peter Hasenclever, merchant; formerly one of the proprietors of the iron works pot-ash manufactory, &c. established, and successfully carried on under his direction, in the provinces of New York, and New Jersey, in North America, 'till November 1766: In which the conduct of the trustees of that undertaking, in the dismission of the said Peter Hasenclever, and their unprecedented proceedings against him in America, and in the Court of Chancery, since his return to England are exposed. This case is humbly submitted to the consideration of the King, and both houses of Parliament, to whom the much-injured complainant looks up for redress.

The Ringwood Company donated the Long Pond property to New Jersey in 1957. Long Pond Ironworks State Park opened 30 years later in 1987, when the Monksville Dam and Reservoir were completed. In 1999, the nonprofit Friends of Long Pond Ironworks opened a museum in the park's Olde Country Store. They now give tours of the Long Pond Ironworks Historic District, and have been working with the state to restore some of the park's other historic structures.

Starting at the roadside museum, a mile-long trail leads visitors past abandoned workers' houses to the ruins of Peter Hasenclever's original furnace. Two additional furnaces, now also in ruins, were built during the Civil War. One was called the Gun Metal Furnace, because it was used to make rifle barrels for the Union Army. The other was nicknamed "Lucy;" like ships, iron furnaces were often named after women. Converted to burn coal in the 1870s, Lucy was used until 1882. According to local legend, she was dynamited in 1917, for the climax of a silent movie.

Long Pond Ironworks State Park:
Top: One of a pair of 25' waterwheels, damaged by fire in the 1950s.
Bottom: Blast furnace ruins.

61

Delaware & Raritan Canal State Park: The D&R feeder canal, alongside the Delaware River at Washington Crossing.

Chapter Five

Canals

New Jersey was not always a shortcut between New York and Philadelphia; in the first decades after the Revolution, it was considered a major obstacle between our nation's busiest ports. Travelling overland was slow and expensive, but sailing around Cape May was even worse. Storms and tides grounded so many ships on our beaches that sailors called the Jersey Shore "The Graveyard of the Atlantic."

William Penn suggested building a canal across New Jersey's "narrow waist" in 1676, six years before he founded Pennsylvania. Thomas Jefferson's Secretary of the Treasury, Albert Gallatin, made a similar suggestion in 1807.

The idea also occurred to businessmen and speculators. A canal company came and went in 1804, and two more would rise and fall in the 1820s, all without breaking ground.

The Delaware and Raritan Canal Company was chartered on February 4, 1830, the same day as the Camden and Amboy Railroad. Both companies issued 5,000 shares of stock, selling for $100 each. The railroad stock sold out in 10 minutes, but the canal stock barely moved. Enter Robert Field Stockton of Princeton, a naval officer whose grandfather signed the Declaration of Independence. When it seemed the Canal Company would vanish without a trace, Stockton convinced his father-in-law, a wealthy South Carolina merchant, to buy the remaining 4800 shares.

Before long, hundreds of Irish immigrants were excavating a pathway 50 feet wide and six feet deep, from Trenton to New Brunswick. They also dug a narrower "feeder," to carry Delaware River water through a series of locks to the canal's 58-foot summit at Trenton.

The Delaware & Raritan Canal opened on January 25, 1834. Governor Peter Vroom took a two day tour, and was greeted at New Brunswick with a 24-gun salute. The first boats were towed by mules, at four miles an hour; steam-powered vessels arrived in the 1840s. When the canal was deepened to carry larger boats in the 1850s, its 14 locks were lengthened from 110 to 220 feet. Steam engines, nicknamed "mechanical mules," were installed to work the machinery during the canal's busiest years, the late 1860s.

The canal era was passed quickly. The Delaware and Raritan Canal Company had merged with the Camden and Amboy Railroad in 1835. In 1871, the Pennsylvania Railroad leased these "Joint Companies" for 999 years.

Canal boats carried everything from vegetables to building materials, but during its peak years, the D&R owed about 80% of its business to Pennsylvania coal companies. Trains carried far more coal than canal boats, and moved it faster and cheaper. The D&R began losing money in 1893. At the end of the 1932 boating season, the Pennsylvania Railroad closed its gates for the last time.

The state claimed the abandoned property in 1937. The New Jersey Water Supply Authority now uses the canal, along with the Round Valley and Spruce Run Reservoirs, to deliver water to central New Jersey.

Delaware & Raritan Canal State Park: Griggstown Lock. Locks raised and lowered boats, so canals could cross uneven terrain. After a boat was towed into a lock, gates were closed at both ends. The lock was then filled or drained, until the water level matched the next stretch of canal. Most of the D&R locks still exist, but no longer function. The upper gates have been replaced with dams, and the lower gates have been removed.

The Delaware & Raritan Canal was added to the National Register of Historic Places in 1973. In 1974, Governor Brendan Byrne announced the opening of Delaware & Raritan Canal State Park. New Jersey's longest and narrowest state park, it includes most of the 36-mile main canal and the 22-mile feeder, which parallels the Delaware River from Raven Rock down to Trenton. (There is a gap in the park at Trenton, where part of the canal was built over in the 1930s.) For most of its length, the park is only as wide as the canal and the mules' "towpath." East of

Princeton, both the waterway and the towpath cross the Millstone River in a wooden aqueduct.

From the Bulls Island Recreation Area, where Delaware River water is diverted into the canal feeder, hikers can cross the Delaware on the Lumberville-Raven Rock Bridge. John A. Roebling's Sons Company completed the pedestrians-only suspension bridge in 1947, reusing stone piers built in 1856 for a wooden bridge. Known also as the Lumberville Foot Bridge, this is one of six bridges hikers can cross from the D&R towpath to Pennsylvania's Delaware Canal State Park.

The owner of a mountainside ironworks dammed the Musconetcong River in 1750, to power his machinery. In doing so, he raised the river's source, Great Pond, enough to overflow its banks and merge with its neighbor, Little Pond. The result was a new, nine mile lake that real estate promoters later named Hopatcong.

Shortly after George McColluch came to the United States from Scotland in 1806, he bought a 26-acre farm in Morristown. Like most New Jersey farmers, he longed for an inexpensive way to ship his produce to New York. While fishing at Lake Hopatcong in 1822, he realized that the mountaintop lake held enough water to fill a canal from the Delaware River to Newark Bay.

McCulloch shared his brainstorm with a group of friends, including New Jersey's governor, Isaac Williamson. The state put up $2,000 for a preliminary survey, and then granted a charter to the Morris Canal and Banking Company on December 31, 1824. Crews of Irish laborers began digging in the spring, long before the route was finalized.

Allamuchy Mountain State Park: Morris Canal Guard Lock #3 West at Waterloo Village.

Unlike the Delaware and Raritan, which dropped just 58 feet between Trenton and New Brunswick, the Morris Canal would have to climb New Jersey's mountains to get from Port Delaware (modern day Phillipsburg) to Newark. Boats would have to be lifted 760 feet from the Delaware River to Lake Hopatcong, and then lowered 914 feet to Newark Bay—in a distance of just 92 miles. (Boats on the Erie Canal, which opened in October, 1825, have 363 miles to make the 600-foot climb from the Hudson River to Lake Erie.)

How could a canal climb up one side of a mountain and down the other? In his 1796 *Treatise on the Improvement of Canal Navigation,* steamboat entrepreneur Robert Fulton suggested replacing locks—which could lift boats only about 20 feet—with "inclined planes." The idea was simple enough: float canal boats into wheeled carriages, mounted on iron rails, and then tow them up or down hillsides. Making this work took years of experimentation. Water flowing from the upper part of the canal turned a wheel. The wheel turned a drum, which reeled in chain or rope to raise or lower the carriages and boats. Sometimes the chains or ropes snapped, dropping fully loaded boats down the inclines; eventually they were replaced with steel cables up to 2-1/2 inches in diameter. The canal's largest plane (#9 West) used 1788 feet of track to raise boats 100 feet.

When the Morris Canal opened in 1831, it had 23 planes and 23 locks. An aqueduct carried it across the Passaic River at Little Falls. In 1836, an 11-mile extension connected Newark and Jersey City.

Unfortunately, the canal proved too small for its biggest customers. Pennsylvania canal boats each carried up to 70 tons of coal down the Lehigh Valley to Easton, on the west bank of the Delaware. After being towed across to New Jersey, these boats had to be unloaded. The Morris Canal was just four feet deep, so its largest boats could carry only 25 tons. Larger "section boats," able to carry 45 tons, appeared in the 1840s.

"Section boats" were exactly what their name suggests: boats built in two watertight sections. Until the locks, planes, and carriages were enlarged in 1860, the halves were uncoupled and raised or lowered separately. As a result, the 102-mile trip from Phillipsburg to Jersey City often took five days. (Even after the enlargement, the longest boats—70-ton coal carriers, 87 feet long and 10 feet wide—had to be hinged in the middle, to ease their transition from rails to water at the tops of the planes.)

Stephens State Park: Morris Canal Guard Lock #5 West, alongside the 1930s Saxton Falls dam on the Musconetcong River (guard locks maintained an even water level along the canal). The lock was partly filled in, and its gates were removed, when the canal was drained in 1924. The lock tender's house was used as a tavern until the 1990s.

Like the D&R, the Morris Canal began losing business to railroads in the late 1860s. The Lehigh Valley Railroad leased the canal in 1871, and asked the state for permission to close it in 1888. New Jersey assumed ownership in 1922, after decades of declining traffic, neglect, and political and financial maneuvering. The canal was drained and abandoned in 1924, and the crumbling Little Falls aqueduct was dynamited the following year.

Allamuchy Mountain State Park preserved Plane 4 West and Guard Lock 3 West as part of Waterloo Village. Although the Village has been closed for several years, the Canal Society of New Jersey sponsors occasional tours, demonstrations, and boat rides.

Hopatcong State Park: Lake Hopatcong outlet dam. The first dam at this spot created Lake Hopatcong. A second, built in 1827, controlled the flow of water from the lake into the Morris Canal.

Hopatcong State Park has a Morris Canal museum in a restored lock tender's house. The canal's owners supplied housing because the tenders needed to live where they worked—they were on duty from five in the morning until nine at night, six days a week (the canal closed on Sundays).

The museum overlooks a short feeder canal, which carried Hopatcong's waters to the main canal. In the canal's later years, a lock gave pleasure boaters access to the lake (the lock was replaced by a dam when the canal was drained).

The Morris Canal and Banking Company built a dam in 1827, which raised Lake Hopatcong five feet. By 1900, the lake was a popular vacation spot, served by several railroads and surrounded by cottages, estates, and more than 40 hotels. Tourist guides, such as 1905's *Lake Hopatcong Illustrated*, were packed with ads for hotels, restaurants, and steamboat lines. (They also offered helpful advice: "It is wise not to go in bathing until two hours after eating, three may be better.") From 1925 until 1983, visitors rode roller coasters and other attractions at the lake's Bertrand Island Amusement Park.

Inventor Hudson Maxim bought three miles of lakeshore in 1897, after selling his explosives patents to the DuPont Company. (Maxim's inventions included smokeless powder; his brother Hiram invented the Maxim gun, an early machine gun.) In 1913, Maxim self-published a book titled *LAKE HOPATCONG THE BEAUTIFUL: A PLEA for its Dedication as a Public Park and for its Preservation as a Pleasure and Health Resort for the Benefit of all the People*. In the introduction, he warned:

> *Lake Hopatcong is threatened with ruination; the prosperous communities around it are threatened with extinction, and our most precious mountain-lake resort is in imminent danger of being wiped off the map.*

Although the Lehigh Valley Railroad had been trying to close the canal since 1888, several groups wanted to keep the waterway open. Some of the canal's backers still believed it could be enlarged to compete with the railroads. The Morris Canal Parkway Association wanted to keep the canal filled as a park winding across northern New Jersey. The State hoped to use the canal to deliver drinking water to Jersey City.

Unfortunately, several of these plans would have required lowering the water in Lake Hopatcong, exposing acres of lakebed and stranding the resort's piers.

Kevin Woyce

Lake Hopatcong: Maxim Pier, early 1900s (from an old postcard).

Maxim called one chapter *The Morris Canal Should be Abandoned*, and explained why it "has scarcely any reason for being" in another titled *Utter Insignificance of the Morris Canal as a Coal Carrier*. (By 1910, railroads were carrying 400 times as much coal as the canal ever could. The Pennsylvania alone carried 66 million tons—as much as 132 Morris Canals.) After explaining how using Lake Hopatcong as a water supply would benefit only 5% of the state's population, he inserted a *Property Map of Lake Hopatcong, Showing Its Wonderful Adaptability for a Summer and Health Resort, and Its Equally Wonderful Lack of Adaptability for a Potable Water Supply.*

His conclusion?

"Just as the State of New York dedicated Niagara Park to its people, so should the State of New Jersey dedicate Lake Hopatcong Park to its people."

Eventually, all the plans for the canal fell through. Lake Hopatcong became state property, as did its smaller neighbor, Lake Musconetcong. The Morris Canal and

Banking Company had created Lake Musconetcong in 1846, as a secondary water supply. A narrow causeway divided it in two, so mules could tow canal boats across. Both lakes are now part of Hopatcong State Park.

East of Lake Hopatcong, the Morris Canal rambled across Morris and Passaic Counties, flowing past Paterson's water-powered mills before descending through Bloomfield and Newark to the Passaic River. After 1836, it met the Hudson River in the Paulus Hook section of Jersey City.

Alexander Hamilton's Jersey Company began developing Paulus Hook as an industrial center in 1804. Robert Fulton built his shipyard here, and ran a steam ferry to Manhattan. Over time, the canal company built a freight terminal and two basins, sections of canal wide enough for the 87-foot, 70-ton coal boats to turn around in. The basins, along with much of the waterfront property the canal company created with landfill, are now part of Liberty State Park.

New Jersey's canals were built to carry freight, but they were also popular with swimmers, sightseers, and canoeists (to avoid paying tolls, canoeists usually carried their boats around the locks and planes). In the 1870s, Newark Sunday School children rode Morris Canal boats to Paterson's Great Falls for picnics. Princeton University's rowing teams raced on the D&R until 1906, when Andrew Carnegie built them Lake Carnegie.

Liberty State Park: The Jersey City terminal of the Central Railroad of New Jersey (CRRNJ) was restored in 2005.

Chapter Six

Railroads

New Jersey families have been riding the narrow-gauge Pine Creek Railroad since 1952. Founders James Wright and Jay Wulfson bought their first locomotive—a 1925 Baldwin—from the Raritan River Sand Company for $400, renamed it Pine Creek No. 1, and ran it for several years on a track in Marlboro.

Reorganized as the nonprofit New Jersey Museum of Transportation, the railroad moved to a half-mile track at Allaire State Park in 1964. (The museum operates independently of the park, is staffed by volunteers, and is supported entirely by train fares, souvenir sales, and donations.)

Over the years, the museum's volunteers have restored a variety of historic locomotives, a caboose, and a Jersey Central passenger station from Aberdeen. In 2004, they took on what may their greatest challenge yet.

Nearly 20 years earlier, charter boat captain Paul Hepler made a surprising discovery eight miles off the Jersey shore: a pair of locomotives, standing side by side on the seafloor. Members of the New Jersey Historical Divers Association found the locomotives to be mostly intact, though thickly covered with barnacles and other marine life. (All the wood, of course, has vanished.)

The history of the two locomotives, and how they came to rest in 90 feet of water, remains a mystery. Railroad historians believe they sank in the 1850s, not long after they were built. Hoping to raise and restore them, the New Jersey Museum of Transportation won legal custody in 2004, and attached laminated notices warning against vandalism or theft. That same year, the History Channel featured the site on an episode of *Deep Sea Detectives*.

Pine Creek No. 1 became the "Ernest S. Marsh" in 1959. Named for a president of the Santa Fe Railroad, she is one of four restored locomotives pulling passenger cars at California's Disneyland.

Allaire State Park: No. 117, built for the Lehigh Valley Coal Company in 1925. After appearing with Sean Connery and Richard Harris in the 1970 movie *The Molly Maguires*, the locomotive suffered decades of neglect. In 2005, No. 117's last owner donated her to the New Jersey Museum of Transportation, where she was restored by volunteers. She has been displayed at the museum's entrance since April 2009.

New Jersey's first railroads were chartered and built at the same time as the D&R and the Morris Canals. The two transportation networks remained linked, sometimes as allies, more often as competitors, until the canals finally closed in the 1920s and 1930s.

When both industries were young, skilled engineers were a rarity, and often worked more than one job. In the mid-1820s, Ephraim Beach—a native of Hanover, NJ—was an assistant engineer on the Erie Canal, principal engineer on Pennsylvania's Schuylkill Canal, and Chief Engineer of the Morris Canal. He also found time to help map the route of the Delaware & Raritan.

Beach left the Morris Canal Company in 1835. The following year, he conducted a survey for the Morris & Essex Railroad, which wanted to branch into Sussex County. Although the line was never built, Beach's survey predicted the routes of several later roads.

Abram Hewitt built the Sussex Mine Railroad in 1851, to carry ore from Andover Mine to the Morris Canal at Waterloo. Mule teams pulled the cars, moving up to 300 tons of ore every day. Reorganized as the Sussex Railroad in 1853, the company quickly replaced the mules with steam locomotives and began expanding into Sussex County. Franklin Forge became a major customer in the 1870s, consuming huge quantities of ore, limestone, and coal, and shipping up to 50,000 tons of pig iron every year.

Rail access to New York brought farmers to Sussex County, where the iron companies had already done the hard work of clearing the forests. Dairy farming proved especially profitable; refrigerated milk cars were not replaced by trucks until 1964.

The Sussex reached its maximum length, about 35 miles, in the 1870s. In 1881, the Delaware, Lackawanna, &

Kevin Woyce

Western Railroad bought control of the company and operated it as the Lackawanna's "Sussex Branch."

Most of the forges and mines had closed by 1900. Farmers began shipping by truck in the 1920s, and commuters and vacationers bought automobiles or rode busses. One by one, the branches shut down. The last passenger train left in 1966.

By 1982, New Jersey had acquired 20 miles of the abandoned right of way, from Waterloo Road in Byram to Branchville (there is still a mile and a half gap at Newton). The NJDEP replaced the ties and rails with gravel to create the Sussex Branch Trail: a wide, level "rail trail" that crosses Allamuchy Mountain and Kittatinny Valley State Parks.

Kittatinny Valley also maintains the 27-mile Paulinskill Valley Trail, which follows the roadbed of the old New York, Susquehanna & Western Railroad (NYSW).

Built in the 1880s to carry coal and farm goods, the railroad stretched from Sparta Junction to the Delaware River, mostly following the Paulins Kill River. When the railroad closed in 1962, the city of Newark bought the pathway, hoping to use it as a conduit for a proposed reservoir. Since the reservoir was never built, the NJDEP began buying the right of way in 1985 for a rail trail. The Paulinskill Valley Trail Committee promoted the trail's benefits to local citizens, who were at first hostile to the plan, and the trail opened in October 1992. Many of the NYSW concrete mile markers are still in place, and the trail crosses the Paulins Kill River six times on old railroad bridges.

Kittatinny Valley State Park:
Top: Wooden "Rail Trail" sign, near where the Paulinskill Valley and Sussex Branch Trails cross.
Bottom: An old railroad bridge carries the Paulinskill Valley Trail across the Paulins Kill River near Blairstown.

Kevin Woyce

The first stretch of the Belvidere-Delaware Railroad, running alongside the D&R feeder from Lambertville to Trenton, opened in 1851—15 years after the line was chartered. An extension to Flemington opened in 1854, and the road was completed to Belvidere in 1855. (Located at the intersection of the Delaware and Pequest Rivers, Belvidere is home to the Warren County Courthouse and a large number of Victorian houses.)

The Pennsylvania Railroad leased the "Bel-Del" in 1871, and Conrail took over in the 1970s. In 1995, the 16-mile stretch from Milford north to Phillipsburg became the "Belvidere and Delaware River Railway," a local freight line. The southern stretch, from Milford down to Trenton, was abandoned. The tracks have been removed, and the right-of-way added to Delaware & Raritan Canal State Park as a rail trail.

In 1867, the Bel-Del established its headquarters in a large new station in Lambertville. Designed by architect Thomas U. Walter (whose stone colonnade overlooks Princeton Battlefield), the building became the Lambertville Station Restaurant in the 1980s.

The Delaware, Lehigh, Schuylkill, and Susquehanna Railroad was chartered in 1846, to replace the canal that carried anthracite coal down the Lehigh Valley to the Delaware River. Construction began in 1850; in 1853, the name was shortened to Lehigh Valley Railroad (LVR). The first stretch, from the mines at Mauch Chunk to the Delaware River at Easton, opened in 1855.

(*Mauch Chunk* is a Lenape name meaning "bear mountain." Founded in 1818 by Josiah White, owner of the Lehigh Coal and Navigation Company, the town changed its name to Jim Thorpe in 1954. Thorpe, who died in 1953,

80

attended the Indian Industrial School in Carlisle, Pennsylvania, and won two gold medals at the 1912 Olympics.)

After spreading across Pennsylvania and New York, the Lehigh Valley Railroad bridged the Delaware to Phillipsburg and built a line across New Jersey to the Hudson River. By the 1880s, the LVR stretched from Jersey City to Buffalo, carrying more than four million tons of coal every year.

The Lehigh also carried passengers. The luxurious *Black Diamond Express* made its first run in 1896, and remained in service until 1959, earning the LVR the nickname "Route of the Black Diamond." (Some travellers also called it "The Honeymoon Express," because so many couples rode the company's trains to Niagara Falls.)

Leasing the Morris Canal in 1871 gave the LVR ports on both the Delaware and the Hudson. Like the Canal Company before it, the railroad quickly enlarged its Jersey City base with landfill. By 1880, the railroad had built a causeway to Black Tom Island, near modern-day Liberty Island. (According to legend, "Black Tom" was an African American fisherman who once lived on the island.) As the LVR expanded its terminal, it filled in the waterway separating the island from the mainland. In 1916, the railroad's pier covered the island and stretched hundreds of feet beyond it into the Hudson.

Two years into the First World War, the United States was still neutral. But on July 30, there were a thousand tons of gunpowder, dynamite, and TNT waiting to be shipped from Black Tom to the Allies; British blockades prevented American companies from trading with Germany.

The stockpile exploded at 2:00 am. People as far away as Philadelphia felt the shockwave, which shattered

Kevin Woyce

windows 25 miles from the blast and collapsed the stone ceiling in Ellis Island's Great Hall. Shrapnel punctured the Statue of Liberty. Seven people died and many others were injured.

The LVR fought charges of criminal negligence by focusing attention on evidence suggesting that German saboteurs caused the explosion. Concerned about this very possibility, the federal government passed the Espionage Act of 1917 and created the FBI. But the investigation dragged on for decades. The German government was officially blamed in 1939; reparations were not agreed on until 1953.

The site of the explosion is marked by a plaque and a circle of American flags, near the Liberty State Park Visitor's Center.

The Central Railroad of New Jersey (CRRNJ) was chartered in 1831, as the Elizabeth & Somerville. The company changed its name in 1849, after buying several competitors, and reached the Delaware at Phillipsburg three years later. Next stop, the Hudson at Jersey City. By the 1860s, legal victories over competing railroads and the Morris Canal Company gave the CRRNJ control over most of the Jersey City waterfront, from Paulus Hook south to Bayonne.

Before building its first Jersey City terminal, in 1864, the Central extended its property 4,000 feet into the Hudson, using tons of New York City garbage for landfill. Twenty five years later, the company built a new terminal, three stories high, with a 300,000 square foot train shed covering 20 tracks and a dozen passenger platforms.

Liberty State Park: Concourse of the 1889 Central Railroad of New Jersey Terminal. Visitors now line up here for tickets to Ellis Island and the Statue of Liberty.

The 1889 terminal became known as the "Gateway to the West." The Statue of Liberty was dedicated on October 28, 1886. The new Federal Bureau of Immigration opened its Ellis Island station in 1892. By 1915, about 12 million immigrants had landed at Ellis. Ferries brought most of them to Jersey City, where they boarded trains for every part of the United States.

Passenger traffic on the CRRNJ peaked in 1929, at 21 million riders, and then fell off during the Depression. Facing bankruptcy, the company closed the Jersey City terminal in 1967, and became part of Conrail in 1976.

Liberty State Park: Interior of the 1889 Central Railroad of New Jersey Terminal, restored in 2005.

The first small section of Liberty State Park opened on Flag Day—June 14, 1976. Two hundred years earlier, the Continental Congress had adopted the first American Flag, the one believed to have been sewn by Betsy Ross. To celebrate, Boy Scouts and Girl Scouts raised all 50 State flags over the new park.

For Morris Pesin, a Jersey City lawyer, the opening was the result of 18 years of hard work. On a summer afternoon in 1957, Pesin had taken his wife and children to see the Statue of Liberty. The only ferries left from Manhattan's Battery Park, so they had to drive the Holland Tunnel into the city. With traffic, the trip took three hours.

Liberty State Park: The Statue of Liberty and Ellis Island, photographed from a riverfront trail.

Kevin Woyce

Liberty State Park: Built on land created by railroad and canal companies, Liberty is the only state park located in an urban area.

On Liberty Island, Pesin noticed two things:

- Liberty Island was much closer to New Jersey than it was to Manhattan.
- The Jersey City waterfront was a disgraceful backdrop for a national monument. The empty factories and warehouses were crumbling, the piers were rotting into the river, and the Morris Canal Basin was choked with garbage.

The following summer, Pesin staged a demonstration for local reporters. Renting a canoe, he rowed to the Statue in less than eight minutes. He then proposed building a causeway from Black Tom to Liberty Island. Although the causeway was never built, his efforts attracted the attention of others who wanted to clean up the waterfront. In 1965, shortly after President Lyndon B. Johnson declared Ellis Island a National Monument, Jersey City gave the state 156 acres for a park. Liberty State Park has since grown to 1212 acres, with open spaces, playgrounds, and monuments; the Liberty Science Center museum; and a privately-owned Marina and restaurant.

New Jersey bought the abandoned CRRNJ terminal in 1973. Liberty State Park's founders championed its restoration, and the NJDEP began running historical programs inside in 1989. On the morning of September 11, 2001, the terminal was New Jersey's staging ground for rescue efforts. Ambulances filled the parking lots, as ferries carried survivors across the Hudson.

By 2005, the terminal building was fully restored (the train shed is still closed). Thousands of visitors pass through every day, buying tickets for the ferries to Ellis Island and the Statue of Liberty.

Ringwood State Park: The New Jersey Botanical Garden.

Chapter Seven

Garden State

Two state parks contain working farms, reminders of the days before shopping malls and condos, when New Jersey earned the nickname "The Garden State."

Lenape who lived in central New Jersey made medicines and red dye from berries they called *ibimi*, "bitter fruit." When Dutch settlers saw the plants growing in the sandy marshes and bogs of the Pine Barrens, they compared them to the necks of wading birds and called them "crane berries." In time, this was shortened to "cranberries."

New Jersey farmers began harvesting cranberries in the 1840s. Whaling captains paid $50 a barrel for the bitter fruit, because it prevented scurvy on long voyages.

Thomas Potter built a Pinelands saw mill along Cedar Creek in the 1760s. He may have given the property its unusual name—Double Trouble—after heavy rains washed out his earth dam twice in one season.

Edward Crabbe bought the property in 1904, and founded the Double Trouble Company five years later. Like Potter and his heirs, Crabbe operated a saw mill, but he also harvested cranberries from the bogs. Needing a large workforce—cranberries were picked and sorted by hand— he built a small, self-sufficient village in the wilderness. Fourteen of the buildings still exist, including the saw mill, school, and store; his 1909 cranberry sorting house; and several workers' cottages.

Double Trouble State Park: Cranberry sorting and packing house, built in 1909. The machine in front of the porch is used for harvesting.

New Jersey bought the Company's land, about 8,000 acres, in 1964, and opened it as Double Trouble State Park. The buildings from Crabbe's day are now Double Trouble Historic Village. The saw mill, sorting house, and several other buildings were restored in the 1990s; the rest are closed to visitors.

Four of the cranberry bogs are leased to farmers, who "wet harvest" the berries each autumn. When cranberries ripen they float, so each October, the bogs are temporarily flooded to a depth of about 18 inches. After being stripped from their vines by mechanical pickers, the berries are gathered into huge "rafts," which are then pushed to one side of the bog for harvesting. (Visitors are welcome to watch the harvests, and can contact the park office after Labor Day for dates.)

Monmouth Battlefield State Park: Old Parsonage Farm orchards.

The 1778 Battle of Monmouth raged across several Monmouth County farms, whose owners' names still mark the battlefield: Craig, Rhea, Perrine, Combs. The fields below the Visitors' Center on Combs Hills were the Parsonage Farm, maintained by the ministers of a nearby church from 1734 until 1835.

John Craig, Jr. enlarged his family's farmhouse in 1770. Eight years later, he was fighting in the Continental Army. On the morning of the battle, his wife, Ann, hid the family silver in a well and rode to Freehold with their daughter Amelia and two slaves. Although no fighting took place on the Craig farm, legend has it that the British used the house for a hospital after the battle. The farm remained in the Craig family until 1943, when another farmer bought it to house migrant workers. New Jersey bought the house in 1965, and the Friends of Monmouth Battlefield restored it in 1993. The fields around the house are still planted with soybeans, wheat, and corn.

Since 1908, four generations of the Applegate family have grown apples, peaches, nectarines, cherries, strawberries, and pumpkins at Battleview Orchards. By 1929, the orchards covered 500 acres. New Jersey bought 100 acres for Monmouth Battlefield State Park in 1965, but the Applegates continue to maintain the orchards. Every year since 1972, they have run seasonal "Pick Your Own" harvests.

Visitors to Washington Crossing State Park can see a colonial "kitchen garden," divided into plots for household fruits, vegetables, and herbs, behind the Johnson Ferry House. Rutger Jansen, who owned a plantation along the Delaware, built the house in 1740, and acquired licenses to operate a tavern and a ferry in 1761. George Washington and his officers may have used the house in December 1776, to supervise the Christmas night crossing and the attack on Trenton. New Jersey bought the house in 1922, and restored it to its 1740s appearance for the 1926 American Sesquicentennial (our nation's 150th birthday). The interior is decorated with period furniture.

Gardens of another sort surround Skylands Manor in Ringwood State Park.

Inspired by the Royal Botanical Gardens in England, Columbia University professor and author Nathaniel Lord Britton founded the New York Botanical Garden in 1891. Built on city property in the Bronx, and partly financed by Andrew Carnegie, J.P. Morgan, and Cornelius Vanderbilt, the NYBG now has more than a million plants on 250 acres.

Washington Crossing State Park: Colonial kitchen garden at the Johnson Ferry House.

Two of the Garden's trustees imported the idea to New Jersey.

Lawyer Francis Lynde Stetson built a country estate he called Skylands Farms in 1891. To landscape the hills around his granite mansion and 9-hole golf course, Stetson hired Samuel Parsons, Jr., founder of the American Society of Landscape Architects. Landscape architect for the city of New York from 1895-1911, Parsons illustrated his 1915 textbook, *The Art of Landscape Architecture, Its Development and Its Application to Modern Landscape Gardening*, with photographs of Skylands.

Stetson was J. P. Morgan's personal lawyer, and helped him to incorporate railroads and the United States Steel Company. He knew the nation's wealthiest and most powerful men, many of whom visited him at Skylands. (In

93

between his two terms as president, Grover Cleveland was a partner in Stetson's New York law firm.)

Stetson died in 1920.Two years later, his widow sold Skylands to another NYBG trustee, investment banker Clarence McKenzie Lewis. Born in Jersey City, Lewis studied in England and Germany before earning an engineering degree from Columbia University. After buying Skylands, he hired another Columbia graduate to design a replacement for Stetson's Victorian mansion.

Ringwood State Park: Skylands Manor is a popular site for weddings and banquets.

John Russell Pope studied architecture in Greece, Italy, and France. In Washington D.C., he designed the National Archives, the National Gallery of Art, and the Jefferson Memorial. For Lewis, he created a 45-room granite mansion in the popular "Tudor Revival" style, based on English architecture of the late Middle Ages and the early Renaissance. For authenticity, he imported antique English paneling, Venetian marble, and 400-year-old stained glass from Germany, Switzerland, and Bavaria. (In the 1920s, you could build a palace like this for $250,000!)

Ringwood State Park: The New Jersey Botanical Garden's half-mile "Crab Apple Alley," lined with 166 trees.

Lewis then hired landscape architects Feruccio Vitale, who specialized in estates, and Alfred Geiffert, who worked on Rockefeller Center and Princeton University, to lay out nine formal gardens. These included Annual and Perennial gardens; Azalea, Lilac, and Peony gardens; a Magnolia Walk, a Winter garden, and a Rock garden with dwarf plants around an octagon-shaped pool. For 30 years, Lewis collected trees and plants from around the world. At times, he had as many as 60 gardeners working around Skylands Manor.

Shelton College, founded in 1908 as the National Bible Institute, bought the 1187 acre estate for a campus in 1953. In 1964, radio evangelist Carl McIntyre moved the school to Cape May, where he owned several hotels, including Congress Hall and the Christian Admiral. (Shelton College moved to Florida in 1971, and closed in 1992.)

New Jersey bought Skylands Manor and Lewis's gardens in 1966, making them part of Ringwood State Park. In March 1984, Governor Thomas Kean dedicated 96 acres around the Manor as the New Jersey Botanical Garden.

Ringwood State Park: Abram and Sarah Hewitt collected sculptures from around the world for their gardens behind Ringwood Manor. The columns are from the old New York Life Insurance building.

Barnegat Light State Park: The Barnegat Lighthouse was lit in 1859, to warn mariners of dangerous shoals around the north end of Long Beach Island.

Chapter Eight

Down the Shore

The Jersey Shore was once a world of sand dunes, salt marshes, and scattered forests. For many years, the only year-round residents were lighthouse keepers. They were joined in the 1870s by the men of the United States Lifesaving Service, a forerunner of the Coast Guard. Hired to rescue the passengers and crews of stranded ships, these lifesavers drilled every day and patrolled the windswept beaches all night.

There have been hotels along the shore since the late 1600s, but most were lonely wooden buildings, surrounded by sand dunes and built for the convenience of sailors or sportsmen. Before the 1850s, when Philadelphia railroad promoters created Atlantic City, the only true resorts were Cape May and Long Branch. Most of the shore's other vacation spots popped up in the 1880s or later, as railroads branched out to the northern beaches and crossed the bays to the southern islands.

Development stalled during the Great Depression and World War II, but resumed in the 1950s, when the Garden State Parkway was built. Today, most of the shore's undeveloped land is included in four State Parks. (Sandy Hook, which the Army occupied until the 1970s, is maintained by the National Park Service as part of Gateway National Recreation Area.)

Cape May Point State Park: The 1859 lighthouse is surrounded by wetlands, nature trails, and beaches.

Two of the shore's State Parks—Barnegat Light and Cape May Point—are crowned with historic lighthouses. Both are "Coastal Lights," designed to be seen up to 25 miles at sea, and both replaced earlier towers threatened by beach erosion and inadequate maintenance. (One of Cape May's keepers used the base of the old tower as a storage building; another turned it into a cattle pen.) The brick towers were even designed by the same man, military engineer George Gordon Meade, and lit in the same year: 1859. Meade also designed the 1857 Absecon Lighthouse, for Atlantic City. He returned to active duty during the Civil War, and in 1863, commanded the victorious Union Army at Gettysburg.

Cape May Light marks the southern tip of New Jersey, and the northern shore of Delaware Bay. There are 199 steps in the cast-iron spiral staircase, but the birds-eye view from the top is worth the climb. On the clearest days, visitors can see Cape May and the Wildwoods, and even parts of Delaware across the Bay. Nearer the tower are the park's beaches and nature trails, and an old WWII gun battery uncovered by beach erosion.

Hundreds of species, from horseshoe crabs to Bald Eagles, pass Cape May Point on their annual migrations, making the park a favorite for birdwatchers. Sea birds and songbirds arrive in the spring. Monarch butterflies and dragonflies head south in late summer, with huge flocks of birds following in the fall.

Since 1967, the Cape May Raptor Banding Project has tagged and released more than 130,000 falcons, hawks, and eagles for long-term research. In 2010 alone, 2587 birds were banded, including three Bald Eagles and 243 Red-Tailed Hawks.

Above Right: One of several trained falcons displayed by Master Falconer Ray Pena at the May 2010 American Indian Arts Festival in Rancocas State Park.

Monarch butterfly, photographed at Island Beach.

Barnegat Light State Park: The park's buildings, trails, and coastal forest from the top of the 1859 Barnegat Lighthouse.

Barnegat Light State Park owes more than its name to "Old Barney." The Lighthouse Service deactivated the light in 1927, when erosion threatened to undermine the tower. Long Beach Island residents and summer visitors saved their landmark by building a wood and stone jetty. The jetty has had to be replaced several times over the years. But without it, the lighthouse would have toppled long ago, and the entire state park, including LBI's last patch of forest, would have washed out to sea.

Designated a state park in 1957, the area has been popular with vacationers since the early 1800s, when mainland farmers nicknamed it "The Campground." Jacob Herring built a boardinghouse for sportsmen in 1830, and in 1881, developer Benjamin Franklin Archer built the four-story Oceanic Hotel.

Kevin Woyce

Island Beach State Park: The tower is part of an old lifesaving station, now used by the park's maintenance staff.

Long Beach Island is 18 miles long. In 1881, its only resort was Beach Haven, at the southern tip. Archer mapped out a competing resort for the north end, called it Barnegat City, and pitched it to mainland investors. In 1883, he built a second hotel: the Sunset, overlooking the bay. Erosion soon forced him to move the Oceanic, and his investors began backing out when Barnegat Inlet claimed their houses. The Oceanic closed in 1914, and was torn down in 1920; the Sunset burned in 1932.

Railroad service to Barnegat City was never dependable, and stopped completely in 1923, after the first auto road was completed. Plans to bridge Barnegat Inlet, connecting LBI to Island Beach, were shelved after the stock market crashed in 1929. In 1948, Barnegat City changed its name to Barnegat Light.

Island Beach State Park: Sandy trails cross the protected dunes, providing access to the beaches.

Island Beach had been in William Alexander's family since 1635, when England's King Charles I granted part of New Jersey to the Scottish Earl of Stirling. Alexander, a prosperous New York merchant, claimed the old family title in the 1760s. London's House of Lords rejected the claim, but on our side of the ocean, William Alexander was "Lord Stirling" for the rest of his life.

During the Revolution, the beach was called "Lord Stirling's Island." American privateers hid in the sheltered coves of Barnegat Bay, and sailed from Cranberry Inlet to attack British merchant ships.

After Alexander's death in 1783, the island was once again called Island Beach. The name has been in use ever since, even though Island Beach has not been an island since 1812, when shifting sands filled Cranberry Inlet.

Island Beach State Park: A walking trail along the bay shore, just north of Barnegat Inlet.

Ten miles of rolling dunes and wind-sculpted forests, accessible only by boat, Island Beach remained undeveloped through most of the nineteenth century. When the first lifesaving stations were built in the 1870s, the only nearby buildings were fishermen's cottages and a sportsmen's hotel from 1815.

A second hotel, built of wood salvaged from shipwrecks, opened in 1876. Five years later, the Pennsylvania Railroad arrived in nearby Seaside Park, then a growing city of sprawling wooden hotels. Summer visitors flocked to Island Beach to hunt or fish, and gunning clubs dotted the bay shore.

Still, Island Beach escaped the first wave of development. The railroad ended at Seaside, so the property was never divided into building lots, the dunes never leveled. When Henry C. Phipps bought Island Beach in 1926, its biggest industry was still harvesting eelgrass. (Eelgrass grew in shallow water along the bay shore. Dried in the sun and packed into bales, it was used to line coffins and to fill cheap mattresses. Blight crippled the industry in 1929.)

Henry Phipps started his career as a bookkeeper for his boyhood neighbor, Andrew Carnegie. The two men became partners in the Carnegie Steel Company, and when Phipps sold his share in 1901, J.P. Morgan paid him $50 million for it. Phipps invested heavily in Florida real estate, funded medical research into tuberculosis and mental illness, and built modern apartments for New York's working poor.

He also built three large houses on Island Beach: Ocean House, Bay House, and Freeman House. The first is still used as a summer home by New Jersey governors. The third was named for his estate manager, Francis Parkman Freeman. Together, Phipps and Freeman planned to remake Island Beach as an exclusive resort, dotted with fine mansions.

The Crash of '29 put an end to their plans.

Phipps died in 1930. Freeman, left in charge of the property, established the Borough of Island Beach in 1933. Because of the Depression, the Borough grew slowly; its population was just 31 in 1940. Freeman was mayor and fire chief. His wife, children's author Augusta Huiell Seaman, was treasurer and tax collector. They eventually leased about 100 properties, but when World War II began, the government evacuated Island Beach (Freeman and his family were allowed to stay as caretakers). The Coast Guard patrolled the shore nightly, and in 1945, the Navy test-fired supersonic missiles from the beach.

Kevin Woyce

Corson's Inlet State Park: Boat dock and bayside beach in the northern half of the park, photographed from the Ocean City end of the Corson's Inlet Bridge.

New Jersey bought Island Beach for $2.7 million in 1953, and opened Island Beach State Park in 1959. The Borough of Island Beach was dissolved six years later, the properties Freeman leased reverting to the state when their original owners died.

The nonprofit Friends of Island Beach State Park, incorporated in 1996, helps to maintain the park, and promotes it with nature and history programs.

Corson's Inlet flows between the southern end of Ocean City and Strathmere. It is named for two brothers, John and Peter Corson, who built a whaling camp on the south side of the inlet in the 1690s. (An alternate story is that the brothers were stranded on the beach by the captain of a whaling ship, as punishment for some misbehavior.) The area where they camped was called Corson's until 1912, when it was renamed Strathmere.

There used to be a Corson's Inlet Lifesaving Station on the Ocean City side of the inlet. Built in 1872, it was badly damaged by a 1924 winter storm. Later that year, the building was moved to the south side of the inlet, where the Coast Guard used it until 1964. It was eventually converted to a private home.

Poet A.R. Ammons (the initials stand for "Archie Randolph") spent the 1950s managing his father-in-law's New Jersey glassware factory. On his days off, he enjoyed walking the inlet's beaches and dunes. Ammons published his most popular book of poems, *Corson's Inlet*, in 1965, shortly after securing a teaching job at Cornell.

New Jersey created Corson's Inlet State Park in 1969, preserving the last undeveloped land on both sides of the inlet. Unfortunately, most of the park's southern half washed away in a 2008 winter storm.

The wooden steamship *General Slocum* was built in 1890. On the morning of June 15, 1904, she left lower Manhattan crowded with more than 1300 passengers, mostly women and children headed for a picnic grove on Long Island Sound. Halfway up the East River, the ship burst into flames. By the time Captain Van Schaik grounded the *Slocum* on East Brother Island, home to a now-abandoned hospital for contagious diseases, hundreds of passengers had died in the wind-driven flames or drowned in the river. In all, more than a thousand would perish.

Investigators found that the ship's life preservers and fire hoses were rotted, the lifeboats were impossible to launch, and the crew had never drilled for emergencies. Von Schaik was sentenced to ten years at Sing Sing, and released after four.

Yet the *General Slocum*'s story did not end that day, though she burned to the waterline. The hull was raised, renamed the *Maryland*, and put to use as a coal barge. On December 11, 1911, *Maryland* sank in a storm a mile off Corson's Inlet. Because the wreck lay in just 25 feet of water, the Army Corps of Engineers dynamited it two months later, so it would not block ships approaching the inlet.

Bestselling novelist Clive Cussler founded the nonprofit National Underwater and Marine Agency (NUMA) in 1979, to locate and preserve historic shipwrecks. (Funded mostly by Cussler's royalties, NUMA is named after a fictitious government agency featured in his "Dirk Pitt" novels.) Unable to find the *Slocum* during a 1994 expedition, NUMA returned to nearby Sea Isle City in September 2000. After more than a week of searching, Shea McLean and Ralph Wilbanks discovered the wreck's timbers, buried under five feet of sand.

Retired Wildwood boat captain and shipwreck expert Ron Sinn has been lobbying ever since for the construction of a monument on one of the Inlet beaches. Although no memorial has yet been built, Sinn has succeeded in protecting the ship's remains; in 2009, he convinced the NJDEP and the Army Corps of Engineers to alter a dredging project that would have destroyed the buried timbers.

General Henry Warner Slocum commanded the Union XII Corps at Gettysburg, and in other major Civil War battles. After the war, he returned to his law practice in Syracuse, New York, and was elected three times to the U.S. Congress.

Washington Rock State Park: The flagpole monument, built by the Daughters of the American Revolution in 1912, stands on the foundation of a memorial tower that was begun in 1867, but never completed.

Hacklebarney State Park: Wooden bridge and stone steps, built by the Civilian Conservation Corps during the Great Depression.

Afterword

Visiting New Jersey's State Parks

I visited most of New Jersey's state parks, for photography and research, between April and October, 2010. Cape May Point and Barnegat Light I skipped, because I had already photographed them while working on *Jersey Shore History & Facts*. In March 2011, I walked two sections of the Paulinskill Valley Trail, for the chapter on railroads.

I prefer to do most of my exploring in the spring and fall, when the parks are less likely to be crowded, and the temperatures are comfortable for hiking. There is, however, one disadvantage to visiting in the offseason, especially in these days of budget cuts: many of the museums and historic sites are likely to be closed. For schedules and hours, visit:

www.state.nj.us/dep/parksandforests

This is the official site of the New Jersey Department of Environmental Protection, which maintains our parks. You can find descriptions of the parks there, traveling directions, fees, and—at least for some parks— downloadable trail maps.

If there is a downloadable map available, I recommend printing it before you visit. Again due to budget cuts, some park offices are no longer staffed on a regular basis; at several, I was unable to get a printed map.

Kevin Woyce

Delaware & Raritan Canal State Park: Griggstown Bridge, crossing the D&R Canal.

If you would like more information than the NJDEP site offers, check out *New Jersey State Parks: Camping and Recreation Guide*, by Scott Zamek (2008, Stackpole Books).

Most parks have trails of varying difficulty. If you're not interested in strenuous hiking, be sure to review the descriptions; that rambling line on the map may wander up one side of a mountain and down the other. For a level walk, try one of the rail trails (but be warned, you may be sharing the path with bicycles and horses). How well the trails are marked and maintained varies greatly between parks, and sometimes even between trails within a park. On some trails, I could almost always see the next blaze or two (blazes being anything from reflective metal signs to faded paint squares on trees or rocks); on others, I sometimes found myself wondering if I had somehow left

114

the trail. Now and then, you may happen upon a stretch of trail that is overgrown, flooded, or blocked by fallen trees.

For safety's sake, always remain on marked trails. The biggest animals I saw on my hikes were deer, but I saw signs at the entrances to a lot of parks, especially in the northern part of the state, warning that I was now entering bear country. And while deer may be harmless, deer ticks are not—they may carry Lyme disease. To protect yourself, stay out of tall grass and brush, and wear long pants and sleeves, even in the warmer months. Remember, too, that seasonal hunting is allowed in certain parks.

Always bring plenty of water and snacks. Some parks do have vending machines or even seasonal concession stands, but better safe than sorry. (Expect to carry out any bottles or packaging you bring in. Waste baskets have been removed from most parks.)

Many state parks are free to visit, year round; others charge parking fees of $5 or $10, but usually only in the summertime or on weekends. Most park tours and museums are free, but expect extra fees at privately owned businesses located within the parks, such as Allaire's Pine Creek Railroad or the Liberty Science Center.

Kittatinny Valley State Park: Midafternoon on a forest trail.

Bibliography

Barth, Linda. Images of America: The Delaware and Raritan Canal. Charleston: Arcadia Publishing, Inc., 2002.

Bebbington, George. Washington Rock is Focus of Renewed Interest. Green Brook Historical Society, 1995.

Bill, Alfred Hoyt. New Jersey and the Revolutionary War. Princeton: D. Van Nostrand Company, Inc., 1964.

Heacox, Kim. The Making of the National Parks: An American Idea. Washington, D.C.: National Geographic Society, 2001.

Kalata, Barbara. A Hundred Years, a Hundred Miles: New Jersey's Morris Canal. Morristown: Morris County Historical Society, 1983.

Lee, James. The Morris Canal: A Photographic History. York: Canal Press Inc., 1973.

Mitnick, Barbara (ed). New Jersey in the American Revolution. New Brunswick: Rivergate Books, 2005.

Mohowski, Robert. The Delaware, Lackawanna & Western's Sussex Branch. *Railroad Model Craftsman,* October 1990.

Tilden, Freeman. The State Parks: Their Meaning in American Life. New York: Alfred A. Knopf, 1962.

Wegner,Herbert. A History of Parvin State Park. Parvin State Park Appreciation Committee, 2005.

Wright, Kevin. A Century of Forest Stewardship in New Jersey: 1905-2005.

About the Author

A lifelong resident of the Garden State, Kevin Woyce grew up in East Rutherford and lives in Lyndhurst with his wife, Carin. His regional history books, illustrated with original black and white photography, include *Jersey Shore History & Facts* and *Hudson River Lighthouses & History*. He speaks frequently throughout New Jersey and southern New York, presenting multimedia presentations about the history of the Jersey Shore, Hudson River Lighthouses, New Jersey State Parks, and the Statue of Liberty.

For more information about books or programs, please visit his website:

www.kevinwoyce.com

Washington Crossing State Park: One of a pair of bronze eagles, guarding the park's entrance near the Washington Crossing Bridge.

Kevin Woyce

Also by Kevin Woyce:

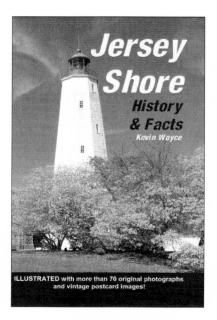

6/15/11